Maria Sigma

Weave It!

15 Fun
Weaving Projects
for Kids

SCHIFFER
PUBLISHING

4880 Lower Valley Road · Atglen, PA 19310

Produced by BlueRed Press Ltd, 2020
Designed by Insight Design Concepts Ltd.
Typeset in Minion, Coop, Neutra Text, and Grilled Cheese

ISBN: 978-0-7643-6065-7
Printed in Malaysia

Published by Schiffer Publishing, Ltd.
4880 Lower Valley Road
Atglen, PA 19310
Phone: (610) 593-1777; Fax: (610) 593-2002
Email: Info@schifferbooks.com
Web: www.schifferbooks.com

For our complete selection of fine books on this and related subjects, please visit our website at www.schifferbooks.com. You may also write for a free catalog.

Schiffer Publishing's titles are available at special discounts for bulk purchases for sales promotions or premiums. Special editions, including personalized covers, corporate imprints, and excerpts, can be created in large quantities for special needs. For more information, contact the publisher.

We are always looking for people to write books on new and related subjects. If you have an idea for a book, please contact us at proposals@schifferbooks.com.

Contents

Introduction 6

GETTING STARTED

Weaving 8

How to Make a Frame Loom 10

How to Make a Hoop Loom 12

How to Make a Cardboard Loom 14

How to Weave 16

How to Make Tassels 18

How to Make Plastic-Bag Yarn 19

FREE WEAVING

1. Paper Cup Basket 22

2. Paper Plate Basket 25

3. Straw Bracelet 28

4. Lollipop-Stick Butterfly 31

5. Branch Weaving 35

FRAME LOOM WEAVING

6. Cloud Wall Hanging 38

7. Plastic Shopping-Bag Clutch 44

8. T-shirt Wall Hanging with Tassels 50

9. Pillowcase Yarn Clutch Bag 55

10. T-shirt Yarn Vertical-Stripe Mat 60

HOOP LOOM WEAVING

11. Plastic Shopping-Bag-Yarn
    Snail Place Mat 64

12. Sun Wall Hanging 67

13. Stool Cover with Fringe 70

14. Rainbow & Cloud 73

15. Dream Catcher with Fabric Pieces 77

Introduction

I first started weaving ten years ago on a DIY frame loom at home in Athens, and at that time it was all about color. I spent hours trying to balance the colors, yarn, and shades until I finally found a new way of "drawing."

Since then, I've found weaving to be an exciting way of playing with color. During my degree in London, I learned how to use a floor loom and basic ways of weaving, and I also discovered how much I enjoy playing with texture.

In this book you will find some fun weaving projects that I would have loved to make when I was a child. These will teach you all the basics of handweaving and will encourage you to develop your very own weaving style. Also, I want to introduce you to the exciting art of upcycling.

You don't need any arts or crafts skills to enjoy my projects—all you need is this book and your own wild imagination!

In your own hands

As you explore your new weaving skills, remember that you are in charge. There's no right or wrong. As long as you like what you've made, it's perfect!

Don't be afraid to find your own ways of making the projects if something doesn't suit you. Feel free to add or remove bits to personalize each piece based on your own style and taste.

Most importantly, have fun! Enjoy the process of making something from scratch—don't get stressed about the end result. If something doesn't feel right, or you don't like it, take it off and try again.

Also, don't lose heart if you make a mistake. Just give it another go!

NOTE TO PARENTS

Weaving is a great relaxation activity for kids—it's a fantastic way to decompress after school or spend a creative day indoors alone (or with friends). Crafts like weaving, with a lot of repetitive actions, are a wonderful antidote to the stresses and pressures of modern living.

With this book, not only can kids create some really neat projects, but weaving in itself is a wonderful learning activity. Through weaving, children can discover patterns and textures, play with color, learn fine motor skills, and develop crucial eye-hand coordination.

With this book you will make sustainable designs that teach and celebrate environmental sensitivity.

Zero-waste weaving

My approach to design is based on the idea of creating beautiful, simple, functional textiles and objects using zero-waste design.

Zero-waste design is not a gimmick; it is vital for our planet. Did you know that roughly 15 percent of the total fabric used by the fashion industry goes to waste? This is just one of the ways that the mass fast-fashion industry affects our environment in a bad way. We all need to be more sensitive and to start thinking of new ways to improve how we treat waste, and come up with new techniques in the art of making things.

But what is zero-waste design, and is it really such a new thing? Zero-waste design tries to create clothing and patterns that leave as little scrap fabric as possible—so nothing ends up going to the landfill.

The philosophy is summed up by the three Rs—reduce, reuse, recycle. We try to use recycled materials and always attempt to reuse materials that would otherwise go to waste.

Zero waste is a quirky name, but it's actually an old philosophy. Throughout history, people have used it for many different reasons. Design driven by function means that people reuse and recycle material in times of need, especially wartime. Historically, women have often made new garments out of the fabrics of older ones. Actually, the very ideas of traditional home quilting, knitting, and sewing very much fall in line with today's zero-waste movement.

In this book I try to provide different ways of creating beautiful things using this eco-friendly philosophy. By using everyday materials that would otherwise go to waste, we can create beautiful and imaginative designs that are aesthetically pleasing, but also truly environmentally sensitive.

Getting Started

Weaving

Weaving is a method of textile making in which two distinct groups of yarn or thread are interlaced at right angles to form a fabric or cloth. This most usually happens on a **loom**.

Looms
A loom is a wooden mechanism or tool frame for making fabric by weaving horizontal and vertical threads together. They come in a wide variety of sizes—anything from tiny handheld frames to huge, freestanding handlooms, and vast automatic mechanical tools.

There are many kinds of weaving looms to choose from, depending on what you plan to weave. In this book, we will use three different types of frame loom for most of the projects, but no loom at all for some free-weaving ideas.

Frame looms are simple looms for anything from basic weaving to complex textile tapestry art. The fixed threads are wound around indentations (or "teeth") on the loom at small, regular intervals.

You can buy ready-made frame looms of different sizes and shapes—rectangular, square, circular—such as the one I have used on page 16. But you don't need to buy one. Just make your own! Follow the step-by-step guides on pages 10–15 to make your own loom with things you probably already have at home.

The job of all looms is to hold long (vertical) threads (called the **warp**) spaced and under pressure, to enable the process of interweaving the horizontal **weft** strands.

Warp
These are the fixed strings that run lengthwise (up and down) on a weaving loom and are always held on tension (in other words, tightly strung). This is what

you'll be weaving onto. Because the warp is wound tightly on the loom, the string should be strong, but not too thick or too thin. Ordinary cotton string is perfect for most jobs.

Weft

This is the yarn that's woven horizontally (side to side) over and under the warp.

The weft can be anything from yarn, fiber, or fabric to even driftwood or shells. I like to use a variety of natural-fiber yarn and/or upcycled materials— some thick, some thin, some with interesting textures. It's all about mixing things up—and this makes it exciting.

To add in the weft, you can use a tapestry needle, a stick shuttle, a wooden bobbin—these can be in different sizes: look at the one I used on page 16 as compared to that on page 38—or just use your hands. As you weave, you can also use a tapestry beater or a fork to pack down your weft to make a denser fabric.

Weft ideas:
Cotton/wool/silk/linen/jute yarn
Cotton/wool fleeces
Fabric remnants
Knitted yarn
Paper and felt strips
Pillowcase yarn
Plastic-bag yarn
Raffia
Ropes and strings
Ribbons
Shoelaces
T-shirt yarn

For the environment's sake, we don't like to use any plastic-based materials, but it's totally fine if these materials are upcycled and not bought. Reusing materials that you have at home is cheaper and better for the planet. Some of these ideas—such as plastic-bag or T-shirt yarn—mean you have to create your own yarn: see pages 19–21 for an explanation of how to do this.

In this book we will explore projects with an artistic approach by breaking some rules, focusing on upcycling materials and having a lot of fun!

How to Make a Frame Loom

Materials
Cotton string
Open-back frame (a canvas stretcher frame, an old poster/picture frame, or an old mirror frame)
Pencil
Ruler or measuring tape
Scissors

For this project I am using an old picture frame as a loom.

1 Remove the glass and the back of the frame—you will be left only with the frame.

2 To start, mark with a pencil the inside top every 0.5 in. (1.3 cm) from one side to the other, using a ruler or a measuring tape.

3 Repeat the same process on the inside of the bottom of the frame.

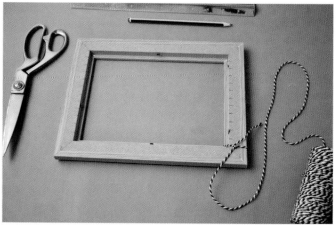

4 Tie the end of your string with a double knot onto the first mark at the bottom left of the frame.

5 Loop the string under and over the opposite (first) mark on the top of the frame, and back down under and over the next (second) mark at the bottom of the frame. Continue doing that by following the pencil marks and making a figure-eight pattern each time, until you have reached the right side of the frame. The strings should be crisscrossed around the middle of the loom.

6 When you reach the right side of the loom, cut the string and make a double knot at the last pencil mark.

> Tip
> Make sure the tension is even and tight, but not too tight, before tying a knot at the top of the frame.

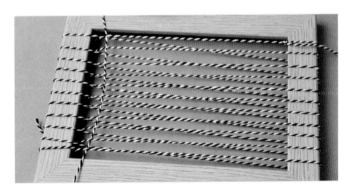

7 Take the end of the string and place it through the strings—under where the strings cross each other.

8 Push the string to the top of the frame and tie it off securely on both sides. You'll immediately notice that the tension is tighter. Now when you introduce the shed rod (the rod that pushes the weaving together), it will separate the upper and lower warp strings, making it easier to weave!

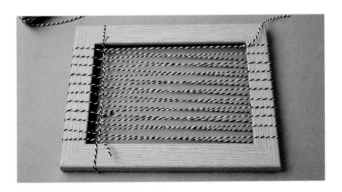

9 This is what your loom should look like. Notice how the warps crisscross above the vertical string. The warp strings are evenly separated—and there is clear separation of a top layer of strings (top warp) and a bottom layer of strings (bottom warp).

What can you make on a homemade frame loom?

Some suggestions:
- bookmarks
- clutch bag
- cushion cover
- pencil case
- potholders and place mats
- scarves
- wall hangings

How to Make a Hoop Loom

Materials
Embroidery hoop
Cotton string
Scissors

I have used a typical 10 in. (25.5 cm) embroidery hoop here. This shape/type of loom is—obviously—best for circular projects such as the Snail place mat on page 64 and Sun wall hanging on page 67.

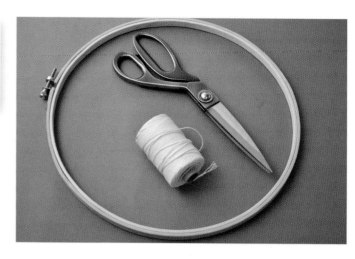

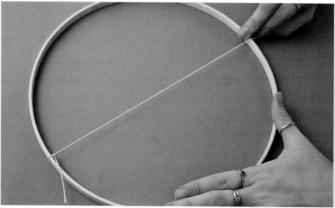

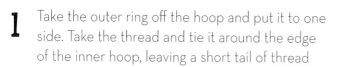

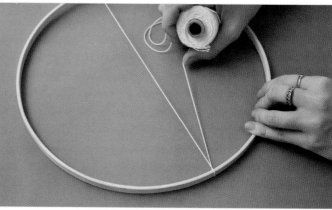

1 Take the outer ring off the hoop and put it to one side. Take the thread and tie it around the edge of the inner hoop, leaving a short tail of thread to tie later. Pull the thread straight down over the bottom of the opposite edge of the hoop. Take it over the edge and to the back.

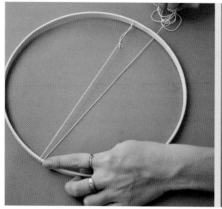

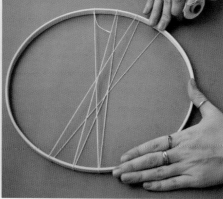

2 The next step is to bring the thread over the front of the hoop about 1 in. (2.5 cm) away from where you started. Continue taking the thread over the edge and up and over the other all the time, keeping the strings about 1 in. (2.5 cm) apart. Make sure you keep the thread taut or it will slip and tangle.

3 Make sure the thread always crosses in the center, until you reach all the way around the hoop.

4 When you have completed the circle, cut the string, leaving about a 2 in. (5 cm) tail.

5 Before threading the last strand, take the thread around the center a couple of times to keep it all together. Take the last strand up to meet the first thread and tie it to the end you left at the beginning.

6 Lace the exterior of the hoop back to secure the strings.

The warp threads are now secure on your loom and you're ready to weave!

What can you make on a hoop loom?

Some suggestions:
- cushion cover
- place mats
- potholders
- wall hangings

How to Make a Cardboard Loom

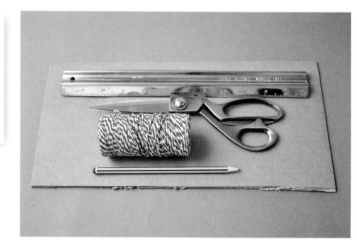

Materials
1 pc. sturdy cardboard
Cotton string
Masking tape
Scissors

Note
Cardboard loom weaving is fun
and easy, and you'll be amazed
with the projects you can make
using just a piece of cardboard
and some yarn scraps.
The advantage of using a
cardboard loom is that you can
make it as small or as large as
you want. Plus, if you are making
a wall hanging, you do not have
to take your woven piece off
afterward. You could leave it
on and hang it as it is—or frame
it. You could even paint the
cardboard your favorite color!

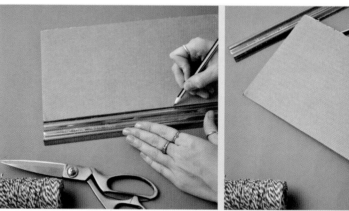

1 Mark out with your pencil and a ruler exactly how big you want your loom to be—then cut it out.

2 Using your pencil and ruler, mark out evenly spaced cuts across one end of the loom You can make as many cuts as you like, but they must be evenly spaced out. Make identical cuts at the other end of your piece of cardboard.

3 Draw a line about 0.5 in. (1.2 cm) under your marks on both sides.

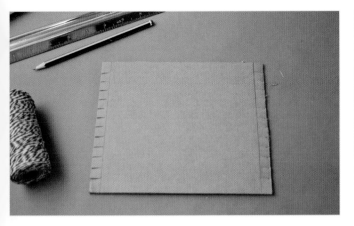

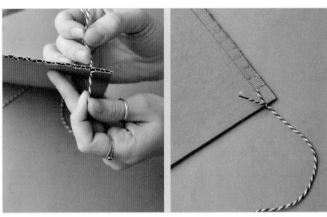

4 Create "teeth" on both sides. With a pair of sharp scissors, cut down all the vertical marks to the marked line.

5 Now to make your warp. Slip the end of the string into the first slit at one end of the loom and make a double knot around the first "tooth."

6 Carry this piece of string down the front of the loom to the matching slit at the bottom, and bring it back up behind the loom to the second slit. This time go around the back of the second "tooth."

7 Pull the string down the front of the loom again, and up the back to the second bottom slit and loop it around the back of the third "tooth." Continue until you have gone through all the slits.

What can you make on a cardboard loom?

Some suggestions:
- cushion cover
- bookmarks
- potholders and place mats
- scarves
- wall hangings

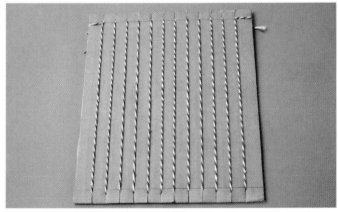

8 Cut your string and double-knot it around the last "tooth," and you are ready to weave on it!

How to Weave

1 To begin weaving, thread a 1–2 ft. (30–60 cm) length of yarn through your needle. There are lots of hobby-weaving kits available, such as this one. They come with either a needle or a wooden shuttle. Both have a large eye at one end for the yarn. A shuttle can also be used to push the weave together firmly.

2 Starting at the bottom of the loom, push your needle over the first warp string and under the second warp string, and then over the third and under the fourth and so on, over and under the warp, until you reach the other side of the loom.

> **Tip**
> Keeping your project under 2 ft. (60 cm) in length will minimize tangles and frustration.

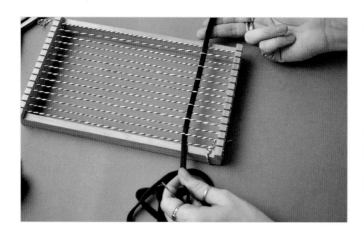

3 Pull your excess yarn so you end up with a short tail on the side you started. You will weave this tail in later on.

> **Note**
> This is your first weft row, and you have been over the odd warp strings and under the even warp strings.

4 Use your fingers to push the yarn to the bottom of the loom.

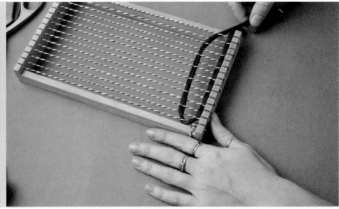

5 Starting from where you finished your previous row, go over the even warp strings and under the odd warp strings—the opposite to the way you did the first row.

6 Before you begin on row three, you need to weave in the tail. Using your fingers, weave the tail on top of row two.

7 Repeat steps 2 and 4 and carry on back and forth across the loom until the yarn runs out. Finish at an edge and leave the tail hanging loosely there.

Remember

Before you continue the next row with another yarn, weave in the tail, on top of the last row—like step 5.

Now you can continue on with the same yarn or change yarn—as you repeat steps 2-7.

How to Make Tassels

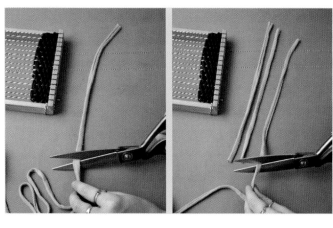

1 To add tassels, cut a bunch of yarn double the length of your desired tassel length.

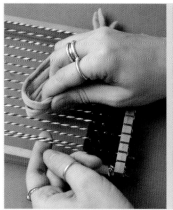 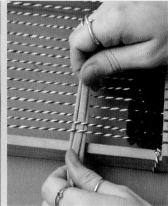

2 Take a group of up to five strands (depending on the thickness of the yarn) and center it under the first two of the top and bottom warps.

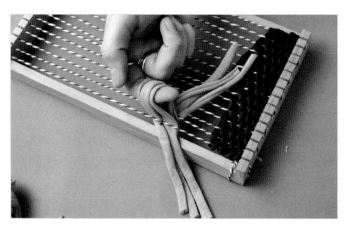

3 Slide a finger under the middle of the bunch between the two wefts. Then pull the center up, creating a loop.

4 Through the loop, grab the ends from underneath and pull tight.

You can play around with the color and the length of your tassels depending on the effect you want to create.

5 Slide the tassel down and repeat across the width of the weaving.

How to Make Plastic-Bag Yarn

Materials
Thin plastic shopping bag
Scissors

Making yarn from old plastic bags is an easy process that can be done in a number of ways.

Tip
It's a good idea to cut strips between about 0.5 and 1 in. (12.5–25.5 mm) wide, but you can certainly just cut them by eye. It's unlikely you'll get all the cuts perfectly straight anyway, and there's no need to fret if you don't.

1 To start making your plastic-bag yarn, flatten the bag so that the sides are straight, with the holes for the handle at the top. You should now have a flat rectangle.

2 Trim off the top of the bag to lose the handles and trim off the bottom seam. Use a long—ideally metal—ruler to get the lines straight.

3 Stretch the bag with your hands. Turn it so the still-intact sides are at the top and bottom (the open ends should now be on the left and right sides). Then fold from the bottom toward the top twice.

4 Cut the bag into strips, from top to bottom, leaving about 1 in. (2.5 cm) of uncut space at the end seam—under the ruler in these photographs. Now unfold the bag so you are ready for step 5.

Tip
To cut the bag so that your plastic yarn comes out in one continuous strip, start cutting at the first front strip of the first loop of the bag.

5 Now we need to cut the strips to form a continuous loop. This is easier than it looks, but you need to concentrate. Cut the space between the first loop and the second loop at an angle, as shown in the photo.

Tip
You can use the same method for making T-shirt yarn, tote bag yarn, and pillowcase yarn. This method works for anything in a ready-made tube shape.

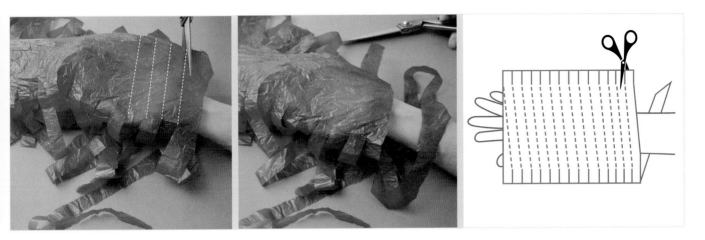

6 Slide your arm inside the bag and open it up so that the uncut portion of the bag is in a single layer. You can wear it around your arm like a sleeve to keep the sides apart and untangled. Cut across the bag from the top to the bottom, following the dotted lines.

7 Continue in this manner until the entire bag is cut into one continuous strip. It might take one or two attempts to get it right, but the process is very simple once you understand it.

8 Wind your strand of plastic yarn into a ball. When you're done, you'll be ready to weave with it!

1. Paper Cup Basket

Materials
One paper cup
2–4 different colors of knitting
 yarn
Scissors

Free weaving is an easy way to weave without having to use a loom. By using everyday objects, we can create really fun designs. Here we have turned a paper cup into an attractive pen pot. You can either use already patterned cups or ordinary plain white ones, which you can decorate before you weave to make a really unique piece.

Everyday objects found around the home can become useful and attractive items with just a little skill and imagination. Start with a simple paper cup . . .

1 Cut the cup into seven equal tabs. You can cut the slits all the way to the bottom of the cup, but I left about 1 in. (2.5 cm) of the cup still intact because I like seeing the base of my cup.

2 Take the end of your first yarn—the bottom layer of stripes—and tie a knot around one of the tabs.

3 Weave a few rows by going over and under the tabs. Keep repeating this over-and-under process as you go around the cup. Soon you'll see a band of color appear.

4 When you run out of yarn or want to change color, simply tie another string on. Cut off the yarn and tie on the next color with a knot on the inside of the cup and continue weaving.

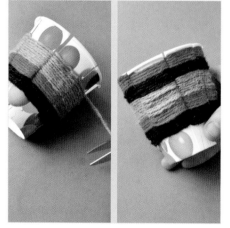

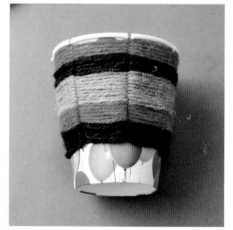

5 Continue weaving and changing color stripes until you reach the top of the cup.

6 When you're done, just double-knot-off your string to the closest tail inside the cup. Trim it, and hide the excess bit inside your weaving.

You have made yourself an attractive container for your pencils.

2. Paper Plate Basket

Materials
Paper plate
2-4 different colors of knitting
  yarn
Scissors

This project really couldn't be simpler—just don't put anything wet or sticky in the bowl!

Everyone needs bowls for all those bits and bobs that litter our desks. Whether it's for your glass marbles or craft items, erasers, or memory sticks, make this useful bowl quickly from a paper plate. Again, this project uses free weaving, so no need for any special equipment. You can choose your colors to go with the decoration or themes of your room.

1 Cut the plate into an odd number of strips, but each to the same length. I have cut my plate into nine regular pieces. Leave a good-sized central circle uncut.

2 Slice small "V" shapes off the edges of the strips.

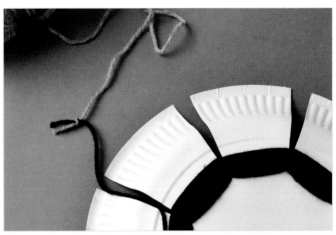

3 Tie the end of your yarn around one of the strips.

4 Weave a few rounds and then cut off and tie on the next color of yarn.

5 Continue weaving and creating color stripes with the yarn.

6 Chop off any long tails and hide them in between the woven yarn by pushing them in with your fingers.

And your new basket is ready!

3. Straw Bracelet

Materials
Cotton string
2 pcs. colored yarn
2 paper straws
Scissors

These make really cool friendship bracelets and are quick and easy to make. Make lots of them and give them out to all your friends.

This is a really great project to reuse straws. Layer them in lots of different colors! A lovely personal gift to give to your bff!

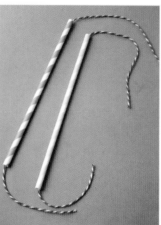

1 Pull the string through the straw and cut it. Make sure you leave tails of about 2 in. (6 cm) on both sides. Repeat with the second straw.

2 Tie the two strings together on one side.

3 Tie the two colors of yarn on top of the knot.

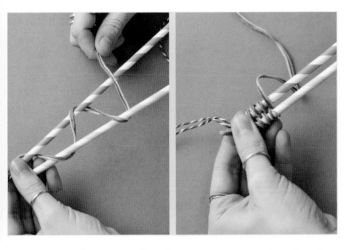

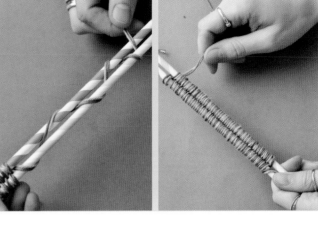

4 Weave them together by going over and under the straws.

5 Keep on weaving until it's long enough to go around your hand.

6 When you have finished weaving, pull both straws out. IMPORTANT: Hold on to the woven yarn with your fingers. Don't let them fall apart.

7 Cut off any excess yarn, but leave sufficient length so you can tie them up together.

8 Knot together at each end the two weaving yarns and the cotton string.

A beautiful bracelet for you or a gift for special friends—make matching ones for everyone!

4. Lollipop-Stick Butterfly

Materials
2 beads
2 lollipop sticks
2 pcs. yarn/string/ribbon
Scissors
Wire

Just two lollipop sticks are a really fun way to make a butterfly and with that introduce extra color into your bedroom. Pick colors that work with your room, and make as many as you need to fill your space.

These butterflies are a really fun way to jazz up your room. When you've made a few, you can hang them from your lampshade—make sure you get an adult to help—or stick them to your walls or curtains and move them around from time to time as the fancy takes you!

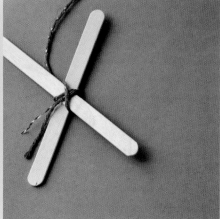

1 Hold the sticks with your fingers so they form an "X" shape. Then, using your finest yarn/string/ribbon, go around the meeting point from all sides to secure the "X."

Tip
Leave a short tail in order to tie up the end of your yarn/string/ribbon when you have finished the weaving.

2 When you have wrapped enough yarn around the meeting point to stop it from slipping, start weaving one side by going over and under the sticks.

3 Repeat on the opposite side so they match. If you change color here, try to keep the changes the same so they balance visually.

4 When you have covered almost half the stick, cut your yarn/string/ribbon and tie a knot with the tail you left in the beginning.

5 Add your next color by first tying it to one of the sticks. Then weave one side of the butterfly with it, then the other side.

Tip

Leave a tail in your first knot so you can tie the ends together at the back when you've finished weaving.

6 Chop off the tails.

7 Repeat on the other side, keeping the color balance the same.

8 Straighten up your wire. You may need to double or triple it—or fold it a number of times depending on its thickness. Then wrap the middle of the wire around the meeting point of the sticks.

9 With your fingers, twist together the ends of the antenna wire for about 0.5 in. (13 mm).

11 Repeat the same at the other end of the wire. Spread the antenna out into a "Y" shape.

You can hang these fabulous butterflies from your lampshades or curtain rods—or pin them onto your curtains.

10 Adding the eyes. Pull a bead through one end of the wire. Fold the wire and twist it below the bead.

5. Branch Weaving

Materials
A "V" shape branch
2 pcs. yarn/string/ribbon/rope
Scissors

Let nature inspire you! Use natural items to make eye-catching designs. You can go as small or as big you wish, but perhaps don't be overambitious the first time! Make sure you choose a branch that is strong enough to withstand the tension that the yarn will put on it.

If you don't have a tree of your own to prune, you could go foraging in the park or the woods for the perfect branch that's come down in the wind. Or you could look around your neighborhood. Chances are, especially in the fall, that someone will be pruning a tree and be happy to let you take a branch away.

1 Tie one end of your string to the branch at the base of the "V."

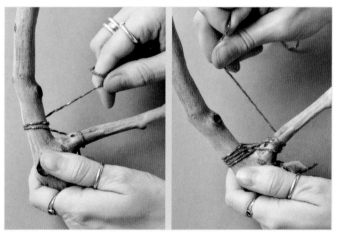

2 Go over and under the two branches. Make sure you keep pulling the string tight.

Tip
To make it very tight and to stop the string from slipping down, every couple of rows or so, go around one of the branches with the string a few times. Repeat the process on both branches alternately.

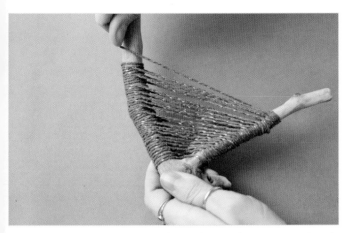

3 Continue weaving until you have almost completely covered both branches.

4 When you have reached the end of the branches, go around a few times and then tie off the end of the string.

5 Cut a small batch of your second color to double the length of your desired tassel.

6 Push the ends in between your woven strings at the end of the bottom branch, and knot the loose ends together.

And your woven branch is ready!

You could make a selection of small ones, or you can make a very big one.

6. Cloud Wall Hanging

Materials
2 pcs. colored yarn
Absorbent cotton fleece/
 pleats
Frame loom
Scissors
Tapestry needle
Warp string

How about an original piece of art for your wall? This is a real statement piece that is bound to trigger questions from everyone who sees it. Don't be surprised if they ask, "Will you make me one, please?"

This is a great starter project for the frame loom. It is quick to make and produces a really great, unusual result. I have used a lovely glittery yarn as well as two plain yarns to really make this sparkle, but you can use anything that works for you.

1 You first need to warp your loom. Follow the steps on page 16 until your loom is threaded for use. I'm using a kit loom here—the major difference being the teeth at each end. These help keep the warp strings in position.

2 Thread your needle with around 2 ft. (60 cm) of string. Note I'm using a long wooden shuttle rather than a darning needle.

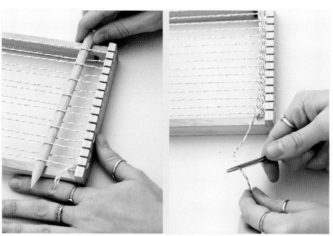

3 Weave in your first row, remembering to leave a tail. Continue weaving. Six rows should be enough. Remember to weave in your tail.

4 Add tassels by combining your two colored yarns and the warp string.

5 Take your cotton fleece and begin to weave it in. Continue until you have a lovely, fluffy cloud shape.

6 On top of the cloud, weave between four and six rows with the warp string.

7 Then push and pack it down with your fingers.

8 When you have finished, lift the tassels and take the work off the loom by unpicking the loops around the teeth on the bottom of the loom.

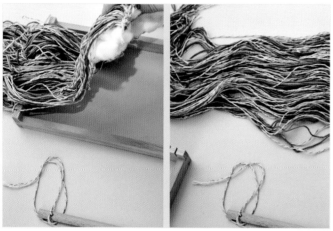

9 Repeat step 8 for the top of the loom. You have now released your project from the frame.

10 Secure your weaving by pulling on the larger loops so the small loops close down. This will tighten the weft. Knot every warp end as close to the base as possible. Tie a length of yarn onto the back of your work to create a hanging loop. Your cloud is now ready for its wall.

TIP
Keep the loops on the back so you can use them to hang your piece.

7. Plastic Shopping-Bag Clutch

Materials
2–3 pcs. plastic shopping-bag
    yarn
Frame loom
Large button
Large sewing needle
Scissors
Tapestry needle
Warp cotton string

This stylish clutch bag is quick and economical to make, so you can make in lots of them in different color combinations and give them to your friends.

This is a perfect project for recycling those colorful, thin plastic bags and saving them from the trash. It is great to reuse materials wherever possible, plus the plastic will keep your keepsakes dry at all times. Eco-friendly, useful, and economical!

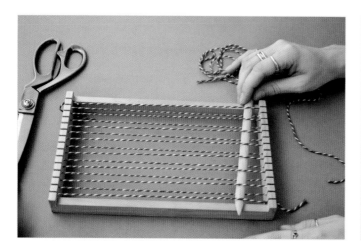

1 Warp the loom with your cotton string. Thread your tapestry needle with the cotton warp string and weave five or six rows. Remember to weave in your tails at the beginning and at the end.

2 Thread the tapestry needle and weave a few rows with your first colored plastic shopping-bag yarn.

Tip
Remember to regularly push down your weave.

3 Cut some yarn and weave a few rows with your next color of shopping-bag yarn.

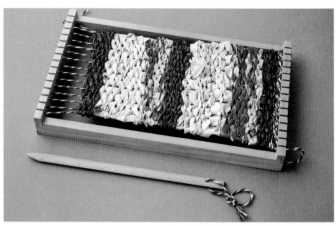

4 Continue weaving some color stripes.

5 When you've finished with your stripes, weave a few more rows with the cotton warp yarn at the top end of your loom. You can now remove your weave from the frame.

6 Cut the warp end that is knotted at the loom and unpick carefully the loops from the "teeth."

7 Turn the piece over to work on the back, and fold it in half. Close this side by tying the warp loops together. Be sure to tie loops from opposite sides.

When you've finished with the knots, chop off the warp loops to leave a short decorative fringe.

8 Now it's time to stitch together one of the sides. Thread some cotton string onto the sewing needle and tie the two ends together. Then start stitching the two sides together. Push the needle into one

side and pull it out from the other. Continue until you have finished stitching it up.

9 When the sides are sewn together, knot your cord to secure the end. Push the needle through to the inside of your bag, Cut the thread and leave a short tail for later use.

10 Stitch on the button at the middle of the top, front side.

11 Thread a long piece of cotton string onto the needle. At the top of the back of the bag, insert the needle through the middle two warp threads and then pull the string through to create a knot. You will use this to close your bag by winding the string around the front button.

12 At the top of the backside, pull the string under two warps, then pull your loose ends through the string's loop. You can now close your bag by wrapping the string around the button.

13 You need a long piece of the cotton string so you can hang your bag on your arm, or wear it around your neck as a necklace.

14 Thread the string on the sewing needle, go through the top right corner, and make a knot with both ends.

15 Repeat the same with the other end of your string at the left top corner. And your bag is ready! Enjoy!

8. T-shirt Wall Hanging with Tassels

Materials
4 colors of T-shirt yarn
Frame loom
Scissors
Tapestry needle
Warp string

We all have favorite items of clothing that no longer fit or are torn or faded—so why not turn these sentimental things into a piece of art that you can enjoy forever. This art project can be scaled up to be much bigger once you get the hang of the crafting.

Create a fab wall hanging by using your old T-shirts—but be sure to check with your parents first in case they have plans to hand them on!

You can make T-shirt yarn in the same way as you make plastic shopping-bag yarn. See pages 19-21 for instructions.

1 This time I am using a frame loom; it comes with a wooden shuttle. First warp your loom with the string. Then weave around five or six rows with the same warp string.

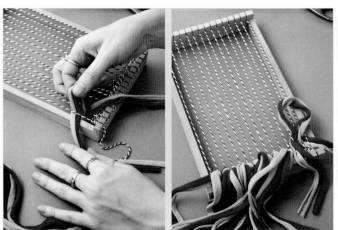

2 Pick your two favorite T-shirt yarns and add tassels by combining them together—here I've used a red and pink combination.

3 Weave a few rows on top of the tassels with one of the two colors you used—here, pink.

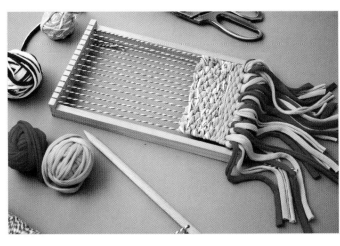

4 Next, weave a few rows with one of the other colors—this time I've used marl gray.

5 Weave a few rows with the other color you used in the tassels, so it's now red.

6 Continue weaving the color stripes; however, now repeat the color sequence backward.

7 When you have finished your color stripes, weave a few rows with warp string to secure the weave.

8 Take your work off the loom by picking out the loops from the teeth at the top and the bottom of the frame.

9 Secure the weft on the bottom by gently pulling the loops on the top to pull up any slack.

10 Secure the weft ends at the top by making knots with the top loops.

11 Chop off the top loops to the length you want, so you end up with a nice fringe.

12 Cut a piece of string a bit longer than the length of your work. Attach the top string by tying it up to the first and last string of your fringe.

Your wall piece is ready for hanging!

13 Slide in your hanging stick or rod, and wrap the string around it.

9. Pillowcase Yarn Clutch Bag

Materials
Frame loom
Large button
Pillowcase yarn
Sewing needle
Scissors
Tapestry needle
Wooden shed stick
Wrap cotton string

This is a great little purse that uses up old pillowcases or strips of cloth leftovers in a novel way. Add a big button to provide a nice bit of detail.

This is another unusual project that uses up fabric that would otherwise go to the landfill. Make up the pillowcase yarn exactly as shown with the plastic bag on pages 19–21. First cut off the end seam, then turn so the intact sides are at top and bottom. Next, cut the strips. Finally, cut the links to make a continuous strip.

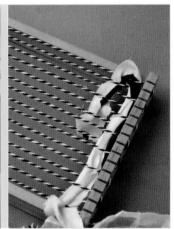

1 Warp your loom with the cotton string. Thread the pillowcase yarn on your tapestry needle and start weaving with it.

Tip
Remember to weave in your starting tail.

2 Continue weaving back and forth until you reach the top of the loom. Regularly push down the weaving with your fingers to firm it up.

Tip
Keep pushing down the weft. This piece needs to be very tight!

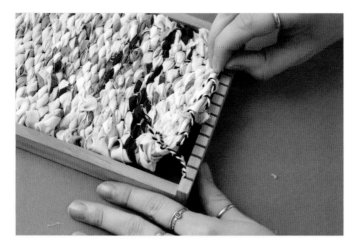

3 When you have woven up to the top, cut the warp strings off the loom and unpick the warp loops off the loom "teeth."

4 Tie up each cut string to its neighbor warp string, at both the top and bottom of the weaving.

5 With your fingers, push down the weft toward the ends, to spread it evenly across the whole warp. Repeat on the underside as well.

6 Cut a piece of warp string—approximately four times your work's width—and thread it to your sewing needle.

7 Turn the work inside out so that the backside is facing you. Fold it in two.

8 Stitch together the top and bottom sides. But before you start the stitching, you need to secure your thread (warp string) by making a knot on the first warp loop.

9 Start stitching the sides together by inserting your needle through the warp loops.

10 When you have been through all the loops, secure your thread (warp string) by making a secure knot at the last loop.

11 Then push your needle out to the side of the work; cut the thread but leave a 0.5 in. (13 mm) tail.

12 Cut some more cotton string and thread it up on the needle. Now stitch together one of the sides—but first secure your thread (warp string) on one of the warp loops.

> ### Tip
> Remember to secure your thread at the end by making a knot at the last warp. Hide the knot by inserting your needle into the inside of the clutch, then cut the thread, leaving a short tail.

13 Stitch together the folded side by going under and around the warp strings.

14 Securely stitch on the oversize button in the middle of the top of the open side.

15 Cut a piece of pillowcase yarn, approximately twice the width of the bag.

16 Using your finger, push the wefts apart slightly on the inside and pull the end of your yarn through. Make a knot to secure it.

17 Now you can close your bag by wrapping the yarn around the button.

10. T-shirt Yarn Vertical-Stripe Mat

Materials
3 colors of T-shirt yarn
Frame loom
Scissors
Tapestry needle
Warp cotton string

This project is quick and easy. The idea is to create striking vertical stripes by alternating the weft colors. When recycling your T-shirts to create your own yarn, try to pick bold color combinations to make your stripes really stand out.

Cheerfully bold drink coasters and place mats are an ecologically sound way of reusing old materials. And they're really useful too!

1 Warp your loom. Cut off the T-shirt yarn into pieces a bit longer than your loom's width.

Tip
Cut more pieces of your favorite color and you can use it as the base color—it's light green for me.

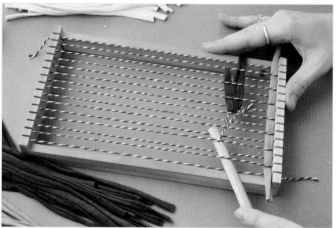

2 Weave in your first row of base color and push it down with your fingers. Leave the tails on both sides hanging out over the edge of the frame. Weave in your second color—here I'm using blue—and push it down with your fingers.

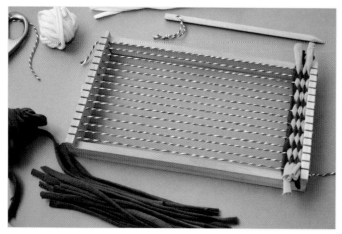

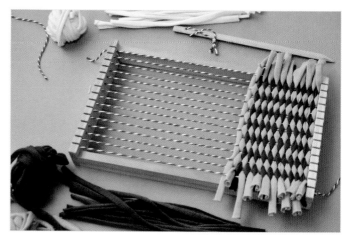

3 Repeat steps 3 and 4 until you have almost woven halfway up the loom.

4 At this point, weave in two rows of your base color, then continue weaving as before, alternating both colors.

Tip
Remember to push the wefts down with your fingers every so often.

5 When you've woven two-thirds of the loom, finish with your base color and start weaving with your third color—this time it's yellow.

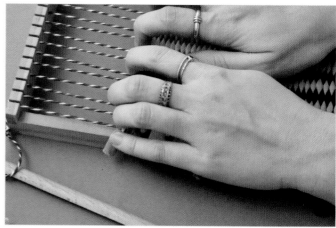

6 When you've woven as many rows as you need, cut off the knotted warp ends and remove the piece from the loom.

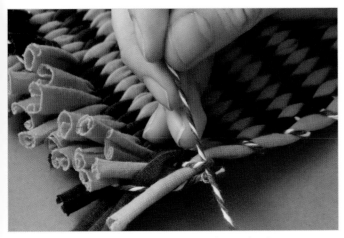

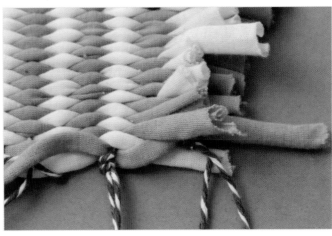

7 Tie each of the loose warp ends to the loop next to them.

8 Pull the top loops to secure the bottom wefts and remove any slack. Then knot them to secure the top wefts too.

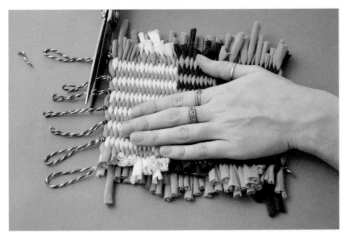

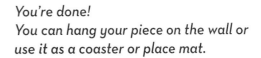

You're done!
You can hang your piece on the wall or use it as a coaster or place mat.

9 Cut off the loops, leaving on a short fringe.

11. Plastic Shopping-Bag-Yarn Snail Place Mat

Materials
3 pcs. plastic-bag yarn
Embroidery hoop
Colored paper
Pen
Pencil and eraser
Scissors
Stick glue
Warp cotton string

Fun projects for recycling plastic bags have never been more relevant than now. Use this technique to make a variety of creatures for both decorative and practical use.

A quick and fun project perfect to recycle your plastic shopping bags. Follow the instructions on pages 19–21 to create the plastic yarn. I decided on a snail, but you can create any animal you like; for example, you could use the finished weave as a bear's tummy!

1 Warp the hoop with your cotton string by following the instructions on pages 12–13. Then begin weaving in the center.

2 Continue weaving by adding more and more yarn of different colors—depending on what you're making, of course. A snail can have many colors.

> Tip
>
> On the last rows, as the warp gaps become wider, you can use double/triple/quadruple lengths of yarn.

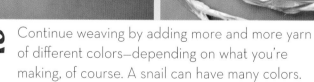

3 Continue until you have filled in the circle frame. Remove the exterior ring and cut the warp loops.

4 With your fingers, gently push the weft toward the center, then knot the warp ends in pairs, to secure the weft.

5 On your colored paper, draw an outline of the woven piece—the snail shell. Using a pencil, draw the snail's body, then cut out the snail shape.

6 Put some glue on the shell area on the paper and place the woven piece on top—the right way up! If you want to make the snail sturdier, use a heavy card, or trace and add a backing of cardboard from an old box.

7 Using a pen, draw the face, eyes, and mouth—then with the eraser, remove any obvious pencil marks left behind. You can always add pom-poms to decorate your design and pipe cleaners for the antennae.

12. Sun Wall Hanging

Materials
3-6 pcs. yellow/orange yarn/
  fabric/ribbon
Embroidery hoop
Scissors
Warp cotton string

Bring on the sunshine with this brilliant sun disk wall hanging. Make it any size you want—the bigger the better!

This is a simple but effective weave using T-shirt yarn; see pages 19–21 to create your own. Try to use strong sunshine colors so it will really stand out. It would be a lovely, bright addition to any bedroom wall.

1 Warp your hoop with cotton string as shown (see pages 12–13). Then start weaving, beginning with your most vibrant orange for the center.

2 Continue with the rest of the orange yarn, working from the darkest to the lightest. Then move on to using the yellows, again working from the darkest to the brightest. When you have woven the whole ring, remove the outer ring of the embroidery hoop.

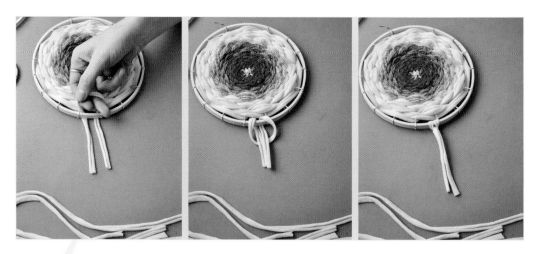

3 Cut off some pieces of the brightest yellow yarn to turn into tassels to radiate around the ring. Use slightly differing lengths for best effect.

4 Continue adding tassels until you have filled the whole ring all the way around.

5 Finally, add a longer tassel, and knot its loose ends together. Use this loop to hang up your sun.

13. Stool Cover with Fringe

Materials

2–3 pcs. T-shirt yarn
Cotton/linen rope
Embroidery hoop
Pcs. of fabric/ribbon
Scissors

Make a hard wooden stool much more comfortable to sit on by making this charming woven seat. Choose the colors to suit your room and enjoy making your weave.

Let's get comfy! Make yourself a lovely soft seat for your chair or stool. Here we are reusing leftover fabric pieces and T-shirt yarn. You must check and see if it's okay to reuse any of these items before you start cutting. It is an easy project to follow and will look great in your bedroom.

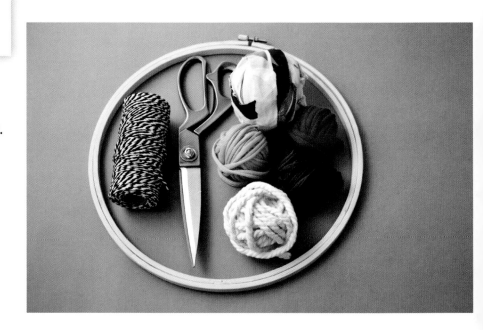

1 Wrap your hoop by following the instructions on pages 12–13. Choose your central color—darkest is often best—and start weaving. Continue to add in bands of new colors to create a pretty design. I've used mostly white, balanced with red, pink, and blue.

2 Make the weave extra interesting by including texture. For this, choose different materials—odd leftover ends of fabric can add unexpected results and prove really successful. Don't make it too bumpy or it will become uncomfortable to sit on!

3 Weave in the rope for a few rows. However, this time, don't hide the tails; instead leave them hanging out at the front. This way you are creating two tassels on the face and thus more texture.

4 Continue to weave your pattern until you get to the outer edge of the ring. Repeat the first color that you used in the center, then for your last row use odd fabric pieces again.

5 Remove the outer ring of the hoop, and cut the warp loops one by one, then tie them together in pairs.

6 Cut off some short pieces of the fabric yarn. Then insert them through the weft of the last row. Knot them.

7 Chop off the tails of the rope to make some nice, short tassels popping out at the front. And you're done!

14. Rainbow & Cloud

Materials
5-6 pcs. colored yarn
Chunky wool yarn (or cotton
  wool pleats)
Embroidery hoop
Scissors
Sewing needle
Tapestry needle
Warp cotton warp

This project will cheer up anyone's day with its bright and friendly colors. To make it even better, you could also add some pom-poms for raindrops!

This is a stunning piece for your bedroom wall and a great project to work up, since it is fun and quick to make. Try using different color combinations to create your rainbow and see what effects you can make. You don't have to be conventional!

Suggestion

If you find it difficult using the tapestry needle, try a sewing needle or even your fingers instead. Weave and work in whichever way you feel comfortable and enjoy most.

Tip

Remember to secure your tails at both the beginning and the end by weaving them in and leaving the ends to hang unseen at the back.

1 Warp the hoop with the cotton string by following the instructions on pages 12-13. This project is woven in two halves: top first, then the bottom. Thread your needle with the first color of your rainbow—here I've started with dark blue. Weave three or four rows on the top half of the hoop only, going under and over the warp end as usual. Cut your yarn, leaving a tail, then move it to the back of your work.

2 Continue to weave, adding in new colors. Remember to move each tail end to the back of your work each time you change color. Weave a few rows with your next color of the rainbow—here it's navy blue—then light blue, yellow, and red.

3 Remove the outside ring of the hoop. Thread the needle with the last color of your rainbow (here I've used pink). Go over and under, around the edge of the inner ring of the hoop so that you wrap its outer edge. Continue until you have wrapped half of the ring, then cut and tie it off, moving the tail to the back.

4 Take the chunky wool and weave in your first row. Then with your fingers, gently pull the wool up in between the warps to create bumpy cloudlike loops on the surface.

Tip

Remember to keep pushing the wool toward the center with your fingers. Keep it nice and tight.

5 As you add more rows, work in between the rainbow itself so you do not have any gaps between the cloud and rainbow. Continue until you have completely filled the lower half of the circle.

6 With the end of your white wool yarn, go around the ring and warp it, so all the wooden hoop is totally hidden.

7 Cut a piece of your last rainbow color—here it's pink—and turn the piece to work on the back of the hoop. Push the weft with your fingers to create a gap, pull the yarn under the ring, and create a loop. Push the loose ends through to make a knot. Knot the end. You can now hang up your Rainbow & Cloud.

Your rainbow on a cloud is ready!

15. Dream Catcher with Fabric Pieces

Materials
1 large hoop ring
1 small hoop ring
2 pcs. colored cotton warp
   string
5–7 pcs. colored ribbon/fabric
Beads/stones
Leaves/feathers
Scissors

Hang the dream catcher above your bed or on your window so it catches the light and the ribbons can dance in the breeze.

This project requires less weaving than the other projects in this book, but it is a really eye-catching design. Use up all your fabric odds and ends and make it as colorful as you can.

1 Wrap the small hoop ring as per the instructions on page 12–13. Cut a length of your second color string to warp the large ring. Don't worry if you don't have enough; you can always add more. This stage can be a little tricky, so you'll need to be patient to get the string tensions just right.

2 Continue to wrap your hoops until they are completely covered with yarn and you are happy with them. Tie off your string to the outer hoop.

3 Pick a ribbon color and weave a few rows on the small ring—not too many.

4 Take a long piece of the same color of ribbon and pull the middle of it under the large ring. Then pull

through the loose ends and pull again to make it tight. This is your central tassel.

5 Cut two sets of long lengths from the rest of your colored ribbons. Try to keep the lengths much the same as your first tassel. Add these to the hoop to the left and right of your first tassel. Keep the ribbon numbers the same so the central tassel stays in the middle.

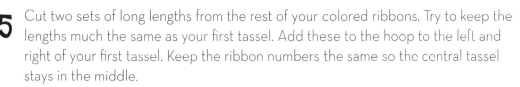

6 Add your beads at the bottom of the tassels and make a knot to secure them. They will weigh down the ribbons and help them hang down—as well as look attractive.

7 Now it's time to add the texture—you can use leaves, feathers, or anything else that catches your eye. Take your outer ring cotton and cut a length shorter than the tassels. Thread your needle and sew through the leaf; tie off the cotton to secure at the back. Now attach your string to the ring in between the tassels. Repeat as required. You can add as many as you wish. Depending on your ribbons, the more the merrier!

Your dream catcher is ready to hang. Find somewhere it can really dance and sparkle!